HOW TO PLAY
GUITAR
FOR CHILDREN
BOOK 1

THE BEST WAY TO LEARN TO PLAY

EASY TO USE CHORD BOXES

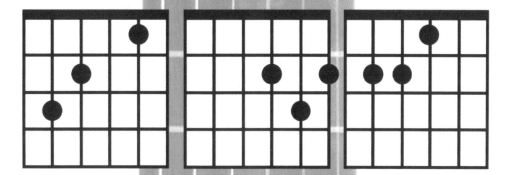

INCLUDES THESE POPULAR SONGS

Mary Had A Little Lamb
If You're Happy And You Know It
Old MacDonald Had A Farm
And More!

James Richardson

HOW TO PLAY GUITAR FOR CHILDREN
BOOK 1

Written and Illustrated By James Richardson
Published By James Richardson

Like us on Facebook:
JRBooks UK

Follow us on Twitter:
JRBooks UK

Email Us:
jimmystrings1@gmail.com

INTRODUCTION

So, your child wants to play guitar and you want to teach him/her?

The only problem is, you haven't got a clue about where to start or how to show them.

With this book **"How to play guitar for children"** I will show you the basics, so by the end of this book you can be confident in teaching your little one how to play some of the best nursery rhymes and popular songs with really easy chord diagrams and lyrics.

Practice makes perfect and by using these techniques on a daily basis, you should be able to rock 'n' roll with family members in no time.

You don't have to sit and struggle with the guitar for hours on end, by just spending **15 minutes a day** and repeating exercises covered in this book, you will eventually be able to progress and play songs from beginning to end.

What are you waiting for? Turn the page quick and let's get started!

THINGS YOU WILL NEED...

Things you will need before you and your child become guitarists:

- A guitar
- A guitar tuner
- Your Child
- Patience

That's all. If you have all of the above, then let's proceed...

PARTS OF THE GUITAR

The image below will show you the names of the main parts of the guitar.

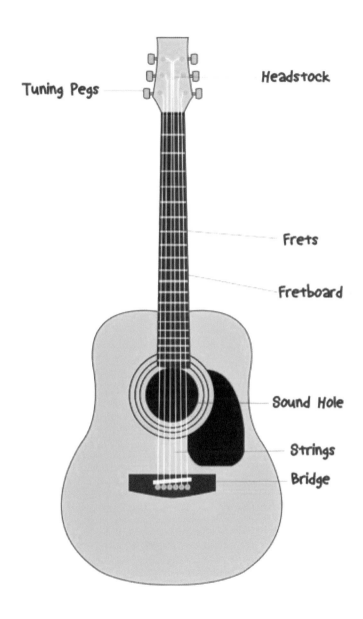

HOW TO HOLD YOUR PICK

I will now show you how to hold your pick. Place the pick/plectrum between your thumb and index finger like the image below.

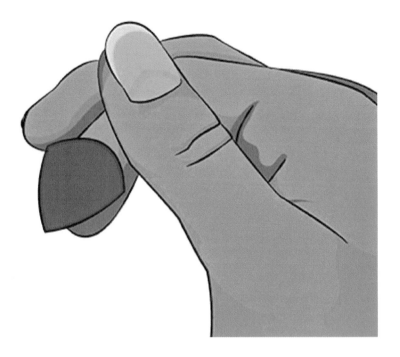

Now place your thumb over the pick. Do not squeeze the pick tight, keep your hand and fingers relaxed. By holding the pick firm, you will restrict the movement of both your hands and pick.

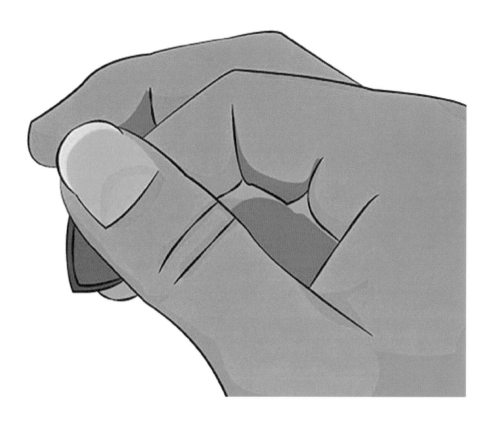

HOW TO HOLD THE GUITAR

There are a number of ways to hold the guitar correctly and these are generally for different playing styles. We will concentrate on the easiest style for you and your child to use. At this stage you do not need a guitar strap as you won't be standing. The easiest way to learn guitar is to be seated. Sit comfortably with your back straight and place the guitar body onto your right leg/lap. The guitar neck should be horizontal and free from any obstruction. Now place your left hand on the fretboard. Your elbow should not be resting on your left leg as this restricts movement for your forearm and hand. Your right hand is placed just over the bridge at the back of the guitar strings. Relax both arms and wrists and try not to be too tense as this will also restrict your guitar playing. Remember making music is a relaxing, enjoyable experience.

Now that you are sitting comfortably, strum downwards with the right hand. It sounds bad doesn't it? What we need to do now is to tune the guitar so that when you strum downwards again it will be a little bit easier on your hearing.

HOW TO TUNE THE GUITAR

Before playing your guitar it should be properly tuned. Tuning is a very important part of learning to play because without it, everything you do will sound horrible and it may make the entire process a chore.

It is highly recommended that you purchase an electronic guitar tuner. These can be bought from any music shop in town or online for a cheap price of £10 and will make your first job of tuning the guitar easier and save lots of time.

Assuming that you have one, I will show you what each string should be tuned to and what the letters mean.

The standard tuning for your guitar is E, A, D, G, B, E.

The thickest string at the top is E. The second thickest string is A. The third thickest string is D. These three strings are your bass strings.

The fourth string is a G. The fifth string is B and the last (sixth) string is also an E. Have you noticed that these strings are thinner than the first three? This is because they are your treble strings.

The bass strings have a heavier, deeper sound and are used mainly for punctuating chord changes. The bass strings are a bit like the strings on a bass guitar and they are also tuned the same.

The three treble strings have a lighter sound and are used to accompany the bass strings. With the bass strings and treble strings both used within a chord, it makes the chord sound more harmonious resulting in a pleasant tone.

The treble strings are also used more in guitar riffs as they have a better melodic sound than the bass strings.

Turn on your guitar tuner. Place the tuner near your guitar, placing the tuner on your right leg just in front of the guitar is a good place. Now use your thumb on your right hand or pick and strum the first E string. The needle on the guitar tuner will start to move. It should go near the centre of the semicircle on the dial and a letter should appear letting you know what the string is currently tuned to.

If the needle is to the left of the centre in the semicircle it means that the note is flat (*b*). If the needle is to the right of the centre in the semicircle it means that the note is sharp (#).

It may take you a few minutes to tune the note correctly but you will soon get the hang of it. To tune the note, turn the closest tuning peg clockwise on the top row of the headstock slowly, whilst thumbing the string with the right hand. Pay close attention to the needle on the guitar tuner and try and get it in the middle of the semicircle on the dial. A red light should glow when you have got the note. Repeat this for the next five strings.

Now that you have tuned the guitar to E, A, D, G, B, E, it is ready to play. Try plucking each string with your thumb on your right hand or your pick. Have you noticed that it sounds a lot better? Good. Now let us learn our first chord.

THE FIRST CHORDS

When I first started to learn guitar, the first three chords I was taught was A, D and E. This was because they are three of the easiest chords to learn and are easy positions for your fingers on the fretboard. These three chords are mainly used in 'blues' music but you can play a vast range of songs from different genres such as rock 'n' roll and many pop songs.

   i.   **The A Chord**

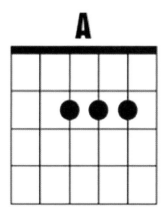

The A chord is one of the easiest chords to learn.

With your index finger, place it on the D string on the second fret and keep it there. Then place your middle finger on the G string on the second fret (directly underneath your index finger). Finally, place your third finger on the B string on the second fret. This should resemble the chord box above. Now strum downwards on the guitar. Sounds good doesn't it? If the strings where your fingers are placed sound dull or are not making a sound you may have your fingers on the fret (the metal piece on the fretboard). Try moving your fingers behind the fret and strum again. This should have resolved the problem and you should now hear a nice A chord. If you don't, pluck each string separately until you have a clear note sounding on each string then strum again.

Once you have practised this chord and it sounds amazing, try not to strum the top string (E Bass). The E string isn't really supposed to be strummed with the A chord but you can get away with it.

ii. The D Chord

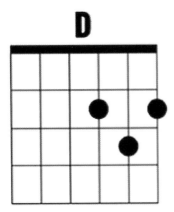

The D chord is also an easy chord to play. It is also an easy chord to change to from the A chord.

From the A chord, Move your index finger to the G string on the second fret and keep it there. Place your middle finger on the treble E string (the bottom one) on the second fret. Finally move your third finger to the B string on the third fret.

Notice that your fingers look like the letter D shape and should resemble the chord box above. Now follow the same procedures as you did on the A chord to get a perfect chord sound of D.

Once the chord sounds good and you are happy with the sound, try not to strum the top two bass strings (E and A). Only the remaining four strings should be strummed for the correct sound of D.

I would recommend that you practice these two chords for a couple of days, swapping between each and when you are comfortable and you are moving faster, then move onto the next chord.

iii. The E Chord

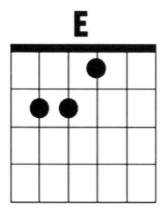

The E chord is probably one of my favourite chords. It makes anything sound good and many popular songs use this chord as the first chord in their songs.

Let's start by placing your index finger on the G string on the first fret. Keep it there. Then place your middle finger on the A string on the second fret and finally place your third finger on the D string on the second fret. Repeat the same procedure as before so all strings are sounding fantastic and strum.

With the E chord, all of the strings are used when strumming so don't worry about missing any strings.

Exercise 1

Now that you have your three fantastic chords lets play your first song. There are many songs that use these three chords and here is your first one. I will give you an easy nursery rhyme first, for you to teach your little one. Enjoy!

Mary Had A Little Lamb

```
A
Mary had a little lamb,
E          A
Little lamb, little lamb,
A
Mary had a little lamb,
E                    A
Its fleece was white as snow
```

```
A
Everywhere that Mary went,
E          A
Mary went, Mary went,
A
Everywhere that Mary went,
E                    A
The lamb was sure to go
```

```
A
It followed her to school one day,
E                      A
School one day, school one day
A
It followed her to school one day,
E                    A
Which was against the rules
```

```
A
It made the children laugh and play,
E                      A
Laugh and play, laugh and play,
```

A
It made the children laugh and play,
E   A
To see a lamb at school

A
And so the teacher turned it out,
E   A
Turned it out, turned it out
A
And so the teacher turned it out,
E   A
But still it lingered near

A
And waited patiently about,
E   A
Patiently about, patiently about,
A
And waited patiently about
E   A
Till Mary did appear

A
"Why does the lamb love Mary so?"
E   A
Love Mary so? Love Mary so?
A
"Why does the lamb love Mary so?"
E   A
The eager children cry

A
"Why, Mary loves the lamb, you know."
E   A
Loves the lamb you know, loves the lamb you know

A
"Why, Mary loves the lamb, you know."
E   D   A
The teacher did reply.

Have fun!!

There are a lot of different songs available for the A, D and E chords of which you can search on the Internet to find. Try alternating the chord progression to E, A and D or D, A and E and familiarise yourself with the chord changes. The more you play the less you will have to think about where to place your fingers and remember always have fun whilst you do so.

THE NEXT THREE CHORDS

Now that you have three cool chords under your belt and are improvising with different chord progressions, I bet you are itching to learn a new one. Next I will show you the chords C, G and F.

C, G and F chords are regularly used in most popular music and they sound very different to the A, D and E chords. Here is your next chord:

i. **The C Chord**

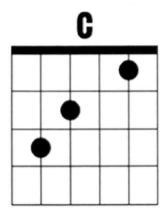

The C chord is one of the most commonly used chords on the music scale. It accompanies nearly every chord and some of the greatest songs use this chord as a base for great progressions.

First, place your index finger on the B string on the first fret and keep it there. With your middle finger place it on the D string on the second fret. Finally, with your third finger place it on the A string on the third fret. This is the chord C. Repeat the same procedure as you did on the first three chords to make each string sound correct. Your finger positions should resemble the chord box above.

Once you are comfortable with the C chord, try not to strum the top string (E bass) as this string doesn't need to be strummed.

ii. **The G Chord**

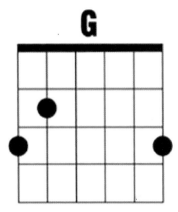

Place your first finger on the A string on the second fret. Now place your middle finger on the E string (top string) third fret. Finally place your third finger on the E string (bottom string) on the third fret. Your fingers should resemble the chord box above.

Practice changing between these two chords before moving to the F chord. Trying to rush through the chords will only slow down your progress.

Once you are comfortable with the two new chords, try adding the A, D and E chords and alternate between them. This will help you to move through the chords and eventually, you won't have to think about the finger positions. When you are satisfied with your progress, Move onto chord number six. The F chord.

iii. The F Chord

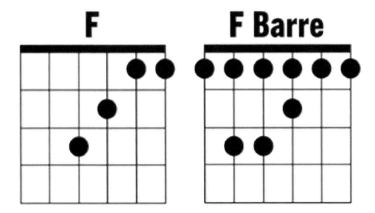

When I first learnt this chord it was very difficult to achieve. Instead of using the normal finger positions, I used the barred version. Barring a chord generally means using your index finger across all of the strings on a fret and then using the rest of your fingers (the other four) to complete the chord. Although mastering the barred technique opens many doors and has lots of benefits, I will show you how to do the normal finger positions for the chord but will give you two chord boxes for you to practice with.

This time, your index finger will hold down two strings. Don't worry it is quite easy to achieve. The easiest way to press them both down, is to bring your thumb up and over the the guitar neck. This will allow for your index finger to easily press down the strings.

With your index finger, place it over the B and E strings (E treble) on the first fret whilst moving your thumb up the back of the guitar neck. Now place your middle finger on the G string on the second fret. Finally place your third finger on the D string on the third fret.

Another way to easily achieve the F chord is to start from the C chord and flatten your index finger over the two strings. Then move your second and third finger down a string.

Practice moving from C to F and eventually you will perfect it.

Add this chord to the other five in your chord collection and practice changing between them.

You now have six great chords to play with. How does that feel? If you search the Internet now for a song you like, you will be surprised that most of the results will include these six chords. It is rare that you will find all six in one song but different variations will be available for you to use.

Exercise 2

I know what you are thinking. You want some more songs to play with your newly found chord catalogue. In this exercise I have given you two songs to practice and to teach your little one.

If You're Happy and You Know It

```
C                         G
If you're happy and you know it, clap your hands.
G                       C
If you're happy and you know it, clap your hands.
F                                 C
If you're happy and you know it, and you really want to show it.
G                       C
If you're happy and you know it, clap your hands.
```

London Bridge is Falling Down

```
G
London bridge is falling down
D           G
Falling down, falling down.
G
London bridge is falling down,
D     G
my fair lady.
```

```
G
Take the key and lock her up,
D           G
lock her up, lock her up.
G
Take the key and lock her up,
D     G
my fair lady.
```

G
Build it up with silver and gold,
D   G
silver and gold, silver and gold.
G
Build it up with silver and gold,
D   G
my fair lady.

I know that I have only given you two new songs but why stop there? Here are some more.

Old MacDonald Had a Farm

C   F   C
Old MacDonald had a farm.
G   C
E-I-E-I-O.
F   C
And on that farm he had a cow.
G   C
E-I-E-I-O.
C
With a moo-moo here
And a moo-moo there.
Here a moo, there a moo,
Everywhere a moo-moo.
C   F   C
Old MacDonald had a farm.
G   C
E-I-E-I-O.

She'll Be Comin' Around the Mountain

C
She'll be coming round the mountain when she comes
(Toot, Toot!)
G
She'll be coming round the mountain when she comes
(Toot, Toot!)

```
G        C
```
She'll be comin round the mountain,
```
F                        G
```
She'll be comin round the mountain,
```
C       G                              C
```
She'll be coming round the mountain when she comes
(Toot, toot!)

One more for you...

There Was an Old Lady.
```
C
```
There was an old lady who swallowed a fly.
```
G
```
I don't know why she swallowed a fly.
```
C
```
Perhaps she'll die.

```
C
```
There was an old lady who swallowed a spider,
```
G
```
That wiggled and jiggled and tickled inside her.
```
C
```
She swallowed the spider to catch the fly.
```
G
```
I don't know why she swallowed a fly.
```
C
```
Perhaps she'll die.

```
C
```
There was an old lady who swallowed a cat.
```
G
```
Imagine that, to swallow a cat.
```
C
```
She swallowed the cat to catch the spider,
```
G
```
That wiggled and jiggled and tickled inside her.
```
C
```
She swallowed the spider to catch the fly.
```
G                              C
```
I don't know why she swallowed a fly. Perhaps she'll die.

Hopefully by now you should have enough information to teach your child how to play the guitar. Children seem to have a low concentration level and by supporting their learning with patience and inspiration, they will soon start to learn with you. Try them with just one chord first such as the A chord and ask them to remember by removing their fingers and placing them back on without instruction. Once they have a few chords remembered, they will get the feel for it want to learn different songs with you.

They probably will overtake you on your learning and one day it will probably be you they will be teaching.

Enjoy every minute learning guitar with your child and listen to music together. This will open their minds to new and exciting music and inspire them to write and sing songs of their own.

I hope that you have enjoyed this book. If you have any questions please do not hesitate to contact me by email – jimmystrings1@gmail.com

Look out for the second book in this series. **"How To Play - Barre Chords for Beginners"**

See you soon.

10009818R00016

Printed in Germany
by Amazon Distribution
GmbH, Leipzig